Stalking

Perspectives on Violence

by Gus Gedatus

Consultant:
Deena Anders
Community Relations and Marketing Specialist
Domestic Abuse Project, Minneapolis, Minnesota

LifeMatters
an imprint of Capstone Press
Mankato, Minnesota

8974

LifeMatters Books are published by Capstone Press
PO Box 669 • 151 Good Counsel Drive • Mankato, Minnesota 56002
http://www.capstone-press.com

Printed in the United States of America

Library of Congress Cataloging-in-Publication Data
Gedatus, Gustav Mark.
      Stalking / by Gus Gedatus.
            p. cm. — (Perspectives on violence)
      Includes bibliographical references and index.
      Summary: Describes stalking, causes and effects of stalking, how to react to being stalked, and how to help others who are being stalked.
      ISBN 0-7368-0429-3 (book) — ISBN 0-7368-0439-0 (series)
      1. Stalking. 2. Stalking—Prevention. 3. Stalkers. I. Title.
      HV6594.G43 2000
      364.15—dc21
                                         99-057553
                                       CIP

Staff Credits
Charles Pederson, editor; Adam Lazar, designer; Jodi Theisen, photo researcher

Photo Credits
Cover: Index Stock Photography/©It Stock International, large; Index Stock Photography/©Charlie Borland, small
FPG/©Telegraph Colour Library, 23; ©Ron Chapple, 50
Index Stock Imagery/13, 19, 59; ©Alona Bollard, 21
International Stock/©Frank Maresca Studio, 32; ©Scott Barrow, 44
Unicorn/©Eric R. Berndt, 6; ©Jim Shippee, 30; ©A. Ramey, 56
Uniphoto/36; ©Mimms, 8; ©Lew Lause, 26; ©Bob Daemmrich, 41, 58; ©Charles Supton, 49

Table of Contents

Violence is words or actions that hurt people or the things they care about. Stalking is a form of violence. It is the intentionally harmful and repeated following or harassment of another person.

About half of victims of stalking are women between the ages of 18 and 29. Both males and females can be victims of stalking.

Recently, several celebrities have been stalked. This has brought widespread attention to stalking.

All stalkers behave differently, but there is a common cycle of stalking.

Chapter 1

What Is Stalking?

Have you ever seen a movie in which one person stalks another? You may have sat on the edge of your seat, wondering what was going to happen. It can be fun to watch such movies because they are not real. They allow you to feel pleasantly scared without being in danger. Neither you nor anyone you care about is really being stalked.

When Stalking Is Real

Violence is words or actions that hurt people or the things they care about. In real life, stalking or criminal harassment is a serious form of violence. Stalking commonly is defined as intentionally harmful and repeated following of a person. It also is defined as harassment, which is the constant annoyance of someone. Some sources define stalking as behavior that makes another person fear for his or her safety. Stalking often is considered a form of domestic violence. This occurs at home or among family members.

What do you think of when you hear the word stalking? You may think about adults who are in difficult situations as a result of ended relationships. In fact, many stalkers and victims are adults. According to a 1997 survey, most victims of stalking are women, and about half of the victims are between the ages of 18 and 29. About 90 percent of all stalkers are men, and about 13 percent are women. Teens can be victims of stalking, too.

About 25 percent of stalking victims get restraining orders against the person stalking them. A restraining order is sometimes called an order of protection, a peace bond, a no-contact order, or a stay-away order. It is meant to protect the victim of stalking.

A stalker may not physically harm a person or damage the person's property. However, a stalking victim's life can be turned upside down, sometimes for a long time. Each year, there are 7 million stalking victims in the United States. Surveys show that 10 percent of North Americans are stalked sometime during their life. All stalking victims have one thing in common: What is happening to them is not their fault.

You may not need information on stalking today or next week. However, sometime during your life you may need the information. The more you know, the better you can protect yourself and your loved ones. This book contains useful ideas if you or someone you care about becomes a stalking victim.

GOODBYE!
I LOVE you SIX TRILLION TIMES.
DON'T you MAYBE LIKE ME JUST
A LITTLE BIT? (You must ADMIT I AM DIFFERENT)
IT would make all of this worthwhile,
JOHN HINCKLEY
of course

3/6/81
1:00am

Famous Victims of Stalkers

Anyone can be stalked. Race, gender, sexual orientation, financial status, or where someone lives makes no difference. Some stalkers target movie and television stars, sports figures, or other celebrities. In most cases, these famous people do not know their stalker. They may not even realize they are being stalked. People who stalk a celebrity they do not know are called delusional stalkers. Delusional stalking will be discussed more in Chapter 2.

A stalker of celebrities usually is unable to form normal personal relationships. The stalker is convinced that he or she must live out an imagined romance with the celebrity. The chart lists several examples of celebrities who have been stalked.

Celebrity Stalking Victims

Victim	Year	Stalker
Jodie Foster	1981	John Hinckley, Jr.

Actor Foster was a young college student. Hinckley attempted to kill President Ronald Reagan, claiming he attacked the president to impress Foster.

Victim	Year	Stalker
Rebecca Schaeffer	1987–1989	Robert Bardo

Bardo saw teen actor Schaeffer on a TV sitcom. He wrote fan mail and tried to visit the TV production set. Finally, he traveled to Schaeffer's home in California. Bardo shot and killed her when she answered the door. He was arrested for murder and sentenced to life in prison without possibility of early release.

Victim	Year	Stalker
David Letterman	Early 1990s	Margaret Ray

Ray broke into talk-show host Letterman's home several times. She even drove his car. She was arrested eight times for trespassing. Each time, she told authorities that she was Letterman's wife.

Victim	Year	Stalker
Madonna	1995	Robert Hoskins

Hoskins claimed he was singer Madonna's husband. He broke into her property several times and threatened her. He was arrested and sentenced to 10 years.

Victim	Year	Stalker
Brad Pitt	1998–1999	Athena Marie Rolando

Rolando spent the night in actor Pitt's home, even dressing up in his clothing. She was arrested and ordered to undergo counseling.

Society's Changing View of Stalking

In the past, law enforcement officials sometimes viewed stalking as a kind of harassment, annoyance, or domestic violence. Publicity given to the stalking of public celebrities has helped illustrate the need for stricter stalking laws. Because of these famous cases, authorities have a better idea of how often stalking happens. They also are more aware of the damage it can do. Law enforcement officials now take more seriously the claims of people who are being stalked.

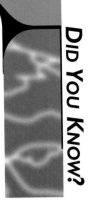
At any one time, it is estimated that 200,000 people are being stalked in the United States. Most of those people are females being pursued by former husbands or boyfriends.

Lawmakers have become more aware of the need for new laws to deal with stalking. In 1990, California was the first state in the United States to make stalking a crime. In 1992, the U.S. Congress helped develop an antistalking law for states. As early as 1993, all 50 states had stalking laws. Canada added stalking to its Criminal Code in 1993.

Laws vary somewhat in terms of definition or approach. However, many stalkers now can be arrested and imprisoned based on a federal stalking law that was passed in 1996. The law prohibits stalkers from crossing from one state to another to stalk a victim. At least nine stalkers have been tried and four convicted because of this law. Sentences have ranged from 3 to 20 years in prison. It is not a perfect solution, but it can be helpful.

A Cycle of Stalking

Stalking behavior varies from person to person. No two stalkers act exactly the same way. As a result, stalking victims can't be completely certain what to expect. However, many experts believe stalkers have a common cycle of behavior. The cycle consists of three phases. These are the tension-building phase, the winning-back or "hearts-and-flowers" phase, and the explosively violent phase. These phases are repeated in shorter time. Each time, the violence is worse than the last.

Tension-Building Phase

In the tension-building phase, the stalker intrudes only a little into the victim's life. The intrusions may include letters, phone calls, or gifts. The stalker may follow the victim or visit the person's home. If the victim is aware of the stalker, he or she may wonder what is happening. The tension builds within the victim. In this phase, the stalker may give up if the victim does not respond to his or her actions.

Winning-Back Phase

The winning-back phase occurs only if the stalker and victim were once in a relationship. The stalker tries to regain the interest or affection of the victim. The stalker might give many gifts or send highly emotional, apologetic letters. If unsuccessful at winning back the victim, the stalker may not remain in the winning-back phase for long.

Explosively Violent Phase

If the stalker's letters, gifts, or calls are ignored or rejected, his or her behavior can escalate into the explosively violent phase. This phase may begin with threats of physical violence, acts of vandalism, or other destruction or property damage. In extreme cases, the violent phase may lead a stalker to assault, or attempt to physically harm, the victim or the victim's friends or relatives. A small percentage of stalking cases lead to murder or to the suicide of the stalker. The violent phase often ends with the stalker being arrested and sent to prison.

"Sometimes I want to be alone. Everyone does. The trouble is I can't stand being alone. I feel like I am afraid of my own shadow. Won't this ever end?"
—Nan, age 17, stalked by her older sister's ex-husband

Points to Consider

How could you tell if you were being stalked?

If a friend told you she or he was being stalked, how would you react?

Why do you think someone becomes a stalker?

Do you think there are more or fewer stalkers today than in the past? Why?

Chapter Overview

There is no standard description of stalkers or their victims.

Delusional stalkers have a fantasy about or a wish for a relationship with their victim.

Teens rarely are involved in intimate partner stalking, but it does happen.

More than half of all stalking cases include people who were once in a romantic relationship or marriage together.

Vengeful stalkers believe that their victim has harmed them.

Chapter 2

Different Types of Stalkers

In the U.S. and Canada, more than 60 percent of stalkers once had an intimate relationship with the victim. Stalkers also may be neighbors, acquaintances, classmates, or other people the victim knows. Occasionally, the victim and stalker have never met. Stalkers often falsely believe they have a connection to their victim. It may be a fantasy or merely a strong wish.

There is no standard description of a person who becomes a stalker. However, stalkers usually fall into one of three types: delusional stalkers, intimate partner stalkers, and vengeful stalkers.

Delusional Stalkers

Delusional stalkers often falsely imagine that they have a relationship with the victim. They may believe this, even though the stalker and victim may have never met. The stalking could begin harmlessly. For example, the stalker may first see the victim riding on a bus. The stalker may start a conversation with the victim while standing in line at the grocery store. The stalker may hear about the victim from common friends in the neighborhood or at school.

In some cases, the stalker may realize he or she has no relationship with the victim. The stalker believes, however, that a relationship will develop with effort. If the victim refuses to have a relationship, the stalker may choose to use threats and intimidation. If these bullying attempts fail, the stalker may use violence or even murder. Delusional stalkers want to be linked with the victim in a positive relationship. If they can't, they may decide to be linked negatively, as attacker and victim.

Studies show that delusional stalking can last longer than the other kinds of stalking. Delusional stalkers may even pursue their victims as long as 10 years. As you read in Chapter 1, many celebrities have been the victims of delusional stalkers. Film and television stars, who commonly play different characters, often fit into a stalker's fantasies. The stalker wrongly believes that a character that an actor plays is the same person as the actor.

According to the Antistalking Web Site, a victim's shame is often the stalker's best weapon. It makes the victim more likely to bargain in an effort to get the stalking to end without a scene. The bargaining continues the relationship between the stalker and the victim.

Case Study: Danisha and Clarence

Danisha worked in a deli. An older man named Clarence often stopped for a few bagels or some potato salad. Danisha was polite and friendly to Clarence, as she was to all of her customers. As time passed, Clarence came to the deli more frequently to talk to Danisha. After three months, she quit her job to avoid Clarence. She was angry and scared. She didn't know what else to do.

Clarence began to mail romantic cards and gifts to Danisha's home. One evening, Danisha and her family came home to find that someone had broken into their home. The drawers in Danisha's room had been emptied, but nothing had been stolen. Danisha's dad called the police. Detectives found fingerprints that matched the fingerprints on gifts Clarence had sent Danisha. The police arrested Clarence, and Danisha and her parents pressed charges. They did not want Clarence to keep on stalking Danisha or anyone else.

Intimate Partner Stalkers

Intimate partner stalking involves people who were once together in a romantic relationship or marriage. More than half of all stalkers and victims fall into this category. Most of these people are in their 20s or older.

Intimate partner stalking may become worse if the victim sees or talks to the stalker one last time. Instead of trying to get the stalker to be reasonable, the victim should be direct in saying no. A victim cannot reason with a stalker.

Some victims want to be polite, so they give time limits, room to maneuver, or excuses. Stalkers may believe that excuses really mean the victim still wants a relationship. For example, a victim may say, "I don't want a relationship right now." A stalker may hear, "We can have a relationship later." A victim may say, "It's just not working out." A stalker may hear, "We can work harder to have a relationship."

Most intimate partner stalkers have low self-esteem. It is often difficult for them to have healthy relationships. Their feelings of self-worth are tightly connected to their sometimes violent power over the victim. They can't bear the thought of losing the person. Cases of intimate partner stalking are the most dangerous. These victims are 75 percent more likely to be killed than other stalking victims are.

Case Study: Connie and Tim

Connie and Tim dated for two years and then got engaged. After the engagement, Tim began putting down Connie in front of others. He became short tempered and threatening. As time passed and Tim became physically violent, Connie called off their engagement. Tim thought that she would change her mind. Every time Connie saw Tim, he only talked about becoming engaged again.

Tim left dozens of messages on Connie's answering machine. He tried to convince Connie's mother to talk her into seeing him. Tim followed Connie for weeks. He commented on things Connie had done, clothes she had worn, or who she was with. At these times, Connie didn't know he had been watching her.

One day Connie warned Tim that she would call police if he didn't leave her alone. She couldn't bring herself to call them, however. When nothing happened, Tim became even less worried about being seen following Connie. She saw him outside the cleaners when she was picking up a sweater. He parked his car for hours across the street from her house. Connie didn't feel safe. She wouldn't go anywhere unless a friend or parent went with her.

Finally, Tim left this message, "Connie, talk with me, or you will not see your next birthday." Connie's parents went with her to the police station. They brought the answering machine message with the death threat. They had other evidence Connie had collected.

The police arrested Tim. He insisted that he would not bother Connie anymore. Connie knew that Tim was lying. She pressed charges, and Tim was sent to prison for several years.

Vengeful Stalkers

Vengeful stalking is the least common type of stalking. Vengeful stalkers do not pursue their victim because of real or fantasized affection. Instead they are angry with the victim and have a desire to get revenge. They feel as if the victim has harmed or insulted them. For example, the victim might be a politician who has helped pass some legislation that negatively affected the stalker. The victim may be a former boss who the stalker feels has overlooked him or her.

One kind of stalking can turn into another. For instance, if a victim calls the police, a delusional stalker's affection may turn to anger and revenge. Perhaps the stalker feels that the victim is trying to embarrass the stalker. Vengeful stalkers try to get even because they see themselves as a victim.

Case Study: Tyne and Paula

All through school, Tyne had always been the best runner. She hoped to get a track scholarship to college. She had lots of friends and got good grades. Tyne was happy.

At the beginning of her junior year, Paula moved to Tyne's school. Paula turned out to be a better runner than Tyne. At first, Tyne tried to be Paula's friend. She felt, however, that Paula was unfriendly and rude. With each new race, Paula's time improved and Tyne's time became worse. Tyne thought that Paula was hogging all the coach's attention. Tyne quit the track team in the middle of the season. She believed that Paula had ruined her life.

Tyne started to make up stories about Paula's dating life, calling her "the slut." For a while, she called Paula on the phone. She would not talk. She just waited for Paula to get frustrated and hang up. Paula's parents allowed her to drive their new red car to school. One day while Paula was at track practice, Tyne made big scratches down each side of the car. She also put nails under the car tires. Paula ended up with a flat tire on the freeway.

Soon Paula saw Tyne everywhere she went. Finally, Paula confronted Tyne, and they began to fight. Tyne pulled a knife and stabbed Paula in the shoulder. Tyne ran off as someone came to help Paula. Within an hour, the police had arrested Tyne. She spent most of the summer in a juvenile detention center. Paula did not know if she would ever feel safe again.

Points to Consider

Why do you think a delusional stalker might imagine he or she has a relationship with a celebrity?

How can talking with an intimate partner stalker encourage him or her?

Which type of stalker do you think would be the hardest to deal with? Why?

Many victims of stalking live in constant fear.

Stalking victims can have physical problems resulting from their fear.

Stalking can affect the family and friends of victims. In extreme cases, a victim and his or her family may choose to move.

Stalking victims may fear being stalked again. They may find it hard to trust other people.

Chapter **3**

The Effects of Stalking

BONITA, AGE 16

Bonita had been friends with Derek since they were in grade school. When they were seniors, Derek wanted to date Bonita. She thought of Derek like a brother and believed he was joking. She wouldn't feel right dating him. When she laughed at his suggestion, she didn't realize how upset he was.

Bonita dated several other guys. After she dated Joe, his locker was robbed. After she went to a concert with Chris, his parents' car fender was dented. None of the guys could prove who had done the damage. However, Bonita knew it was Derek. She felt sad that her friend was so cruel. She was becoming afraid to date anyone else.

Dealing With Fear

While few teens are stalked, it is helpful to know what to do in case it happens to someone you care about. When people become the victim of a stalker, they may feel more afraid than they ever have before. They frequently do not feel safe in public. They may not feel safe even at home.

Fear changes a victim's life in specific ways. Studies show that 70 percent of stalking victims cut back on their social activities, even among good friends. They do this because they are afraid of meeting their stalker. They may feel embarrassed about how they act or appear. About half of victims say that they miss school or work because of fear, sleeplessness, or illness. Three-quarters of stalking victims have problems sleeping. More than 80 percent of victims report jumpiness, trembling, and feelings of panic.

"Ever since we broke up, I feel like he's playing a game with me. The problem is that he is making all of the rules. I feel like I don't have any control."
—Lucy, age 16, about her ex-boyfriend

Stalking and Family Upsets

When a family member becomes a stalking victim, the rest of the family may be affected. They may install more locks on doors. They may change the way they get their mail. They may use the phone and answering machine differently. There may be changes in schedules and curfews. Evidence may be collected to help the police. Family members who worry about the victim's safety may lose sleep or become ill.

Stalkers sometimes vandalize the family's home or other personal property. In rare stalking cases, some families have had to move to other cities or even to a new state. This means new schools, new friends, new starts, and new jobs for the victim's family members.

New Relationships and Forming Trust

Sometimes victims may wonder if they have to change the way they act around other people. Have they become too friendly with people too quickly? Have they misled people about what they want in dating situations? The answer to these questions clearly is no. No matter what victims think the answers are, they should not be stalked. No one deserves to be stalked.

Victims of stalking may be confused, even after the stalking ends. They may feel that they will never have a normal, happy life. If the stalker was a former romantic partner, the victim probably knew and trusted the person. The stalker betrayed the victim's trust. Now the victim may have difficulty trusting new people she or he becomes interested in.

The fear that comes from being stalked may never go away completely. Chapters 4, 5, and 6 describe things a person can do to recover from stalking.

Points to Consider

What do you think causes physical problems for some victims as a result of stalking?

What kinds of problems might a victim's friends and family members have from stalking?

What do you think are the most serious effects that families feel from stalking?

How may experiences with a stalker affect the victim's future relationships?

Chapter Overview

You can look for warning signs in people who could be dangerous.

When faced with unwanted interest from a person, it is important to give a clear no.

You can make your home and car safer.

It is important to keep documentation of all communication with a stalker.

It may be necessary to get a restraining order against a stalker.

Chapter 4

If You Are Stalked

George and Jasmine were in the same English class. Eventually, they went out to a restaurant. Jasmine's friend Rand was in the restaurant. He came over to say hello. George acted unfriendly the entire time Jasmine and Rand talked.

JASMINE, AGE 16

As Rand walked away, George said, "I don't like you to talk with other guys." Jasmine answered, "I'm not going to ignore my other friends just because I'm out with someone." George never apologized. He continued to cut down Jasmine's relationships with other friends. After awhile, Jasmine quit dating George.

Warning Signs

You don't need to live as though everyone you meet is a stalker. However, knowing a few warning signs may help if you have difficulties with a potential stalker.

If someone seems possessive or jealous of time you spend with others, pay attention. For example, George told Jasmine that he didn't like her to spend time with others. Possessiveness and jealousy aren't part of healthy relationships. Some people use their achievements or physical strength to show power over others. Showing power over another person also is not part of a healthy relationship.

"The only time I ever went out with Eddie, he said vicious things about other girls he had dated. Sure, he's good looking. But I don't need to get involved with anyone who talks about people that way."
—Cady, age 17

Idle threats from someone could become real. Some people who make threats actually carry them out. If you react to a threat and are wrong, you may feel foolish. However, it is better to be safe than to avoid feeling foolish.

Someone you are dating may brag about violence toward others in the past. This may show how the person deals with conflict, disappointment, or rejection. The individual may even say, "Of course, I would never do anything like that to you." If someone treats one person violently, the person is just as likely to treat you the same way.

Taking Care of Yourself

If by remote chance you become a victim of stalking, don't blame yourself. Nothing you did justifies someone stalking you. Once you believe that, you can take care of yourself more effectively. Here are some ways to take care of yourself if you are stalked.

Get help from the police or family members. File charges with the police as soon as you feel unsafe.

Tell the stalker no only once. If necessary, say no to the stalker in front of a witness or in a letter. This could be used as evidence if you need to take legal action later.

Ignore the person's attempts to contact you. Any response you make after saying no tells the stalker that you will react to his or her behavior. This is more likely to keep the stalking going.

Many community organizations offer help to stalking victims. If you need such help, call any of the following numbers for referrals to the domestic violence agencies or rape crisis centers in your area.

The Federal Information Center
1-800-366-2998

The National Black Women's Health Network
1-800-275-2947

The National Coalition Against Domestic Violence
1-800-799-7233 (24-hour hot line)

The National Organization for Victim Assistance (NOVA)
1-800-879-6682

Document all stalking instances. Write down dates, times, who you were with, where you were, and any other details you can remember.

Get help from a domestic abuse program before any abuse happens. Preventing physical or emotional mistreatment is better than dealing with it after it happens.

Seek help from a counselor to deal with your emotions. A counselor at a domestic abuse center will have special training to help you.

Call a victim's assistance program. Look in the *City Government, Community Service,* or *Emergency Assistance* section of the telephone book. A victim's assistance program can get you started finding help.

Remaining Safe

In most cases when you say no, the stalker will leave you alone. If the stalker keeps harassing you, you may feel ashamed, guilty, or responsible. That is natural, and you can get help to deal with those feelings. In any case, what is happening to you is never your fault. Following are some things you can do to remain safe.

For Safety at Home

Save all letters and gifts from a stalker. Keep answering machine tapes with recorded messages. If any harm has been done to property, take photos of the damage. All these things are evidence for filing charges.

Document all contact from the stalker. Write down dates you saw or talked with the stalker. Note times of day, what you were doing, and anything else you can remember.

Get a watchdog. This is one of the least expensive and most efficient alarm systems.

Instruct the post office, phone company, and department of motor vehicles (if you have a driver's license) not to give out your address. If your address is not easily available, finding where you live is more difficult for the stalker.

Never give out your home address or phone number to anyone you do not know well.

Change your mailing address to a post office box.

Have your parents install dead bolt locks on all doors and tamper-proof locks on windows.

Get a security system with motion detectors.

Don't discard your mail in the trash where you live. People can learn a lot about you from your discarded mail. Dispose of it some other way. For example, you can tear it up, put it through a paper shredder, or burn it in a fireplace or furnace.

Don't change your home telephone number if a stalker gets it. Use an answering machine to take messages. This will let the stalker think she or he is reaching you. It also may provide valuable evidence for authorities. Some people install a second unlisted phone line for people they want to talk with.

Contact your local phone company about services that can protect you. For instance, you may want to add caller ID to your phone. This enables you to know who a caller is before you answer the phone. You also can block calls to your phone from certain numbers.

Get a free home-safety brochure from the local police department. Some police departments send someone to evaluate the safety of homes.

Let neighbors and friends know you are being stalked. Ask them not to answer questions that anyone asks about you. If possible, show them a photo of the stalker.

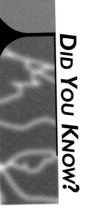
Aggravated stalking occurs when a person causes bodily harm, confines or restrains the victim, or breaks a restraining order.

For Safety Away From Home

Vary your pattern and travel routes for doing things outside your home. That will keep the stalker from knowing what to expect.

Ask someone to go with you to and from school, work, and errands.

If you have a job, ask coworkers or supervisors to screen all calls and visitors.

Get a cell phone and keep it with you at all times.

Tell security personnel at school and your job what is happening. Part of their responsibility is to keep people safe.

Consider getting a car alarm to draw attention to you if you are being stalked.

Each time you approach your car, look for leaks or nails under the vehicle. This can keep you from having a breakdown away from help.

If you think you are being followed, drive to the nearest police or fire station, bank, or hospital. Never drive home or to a friend's house.

Involving the Police

If you are stalked, go immediately to the police. Ask them to notify the stalker of your complaint. Sometimes they may recommend to the stalker that she or he get help. The stalker may feel embarrassed or frightened once you have notified police. She or he will know that you are not going to let the stalking go unchallenged.

Stalking victims should get a restraining order from a local court. A restraining order requires the stalker to cease contact with the victim. However, this is not a magic solution. You may have to pay a filing fee for the order. Also, it allows the police to act only after the stalker breaks the order. However, at least the order allows the police to act. To get a restraining order, contact your local police department. If they can't help you, call the county attorney's office. Many domestic violence programs can write a restraining order, too.

Points to Consider

Why do you think a stalking victim might need a witness that he or she is being stalked?

Why do you think a stalking victim might feel guilty or ashamed about being stalked?

Why do you think a stalking victim should immediately get a restraining order? Explain.

What do you think are the most important things a victim can do in dealing with a stalker? Why?

Friends and relatives can offer valuable support to stalking victims.

It is important to remember that the victim is not at fault.

Remember your own safety while helping a stalking victim.

If a friend or loved one is the victim of a stalker you know, do not accept any letters, gifts, or messages for the victim.

Chapter 5

If a Friend or a Loved One Is Stalked

Annie liked swimming at a local recreation center. A lifeguard named Jeff was friendly to her. At first, Annie was flattered. When Jeff started watching her in other places, she became frightened. Her friends thought she was being silly, but Jeff gave Annie the creeps. She felt she had to tell her parents.

Annie's dad started watching out for Jeff. He was concerned about his daughter's safety. One night, her dad found Jeff peeping in through Annie's bedroom window. He called Jeff's parents and told them about their son's behavior. Annie's family didn't know what they told Jeff, but he stopped stalking Annie.

ANNIE, AGE 15

Be the Greatest Help Possible

Friends and relatives may feel helpless because they can't offer complete protection to someone who is being stalked. You can help in many ways if a friend or loved one becomes the victim of a stalker. As you consider ways you can help, think about some of these things.

Remind the victim that she or he is not to blame for the stalking.

Believe the victim.

Don't blame the victim for what is happening

Don't underestimate the seriousness of the situation.

Offer to help create a safety plan.

Offer to keep backup clothing and personal items at your house.

Help the victim find alternative housing if necessary.

Help the victim list people who can be called in an emergency. Keep a copy of the list for yourself.

Suggest agencies that may be able to help, like a domestic abuse program. Ask for ways you can help the victim.

Be careful what you tell people about the victim's whereabouts, phone number, or travel plans. Even the most innocent information could help the stalker.

Act as a witness to the stalking. You can provide valuable evidence if the victim decides to press charges.

Document all contact from the stalker. Write down dates you saw or talked with the stalker. Note times of day, what you were doing, and anything else you can remember.

If the stalker contacts you, call the police and tell the victim.

Offer to answer the phone if the victim is worried the stalker may call.

If the victim is a coworker, suggest that the receptionist take his or her calls at work.

Tell other relatives, neighbors, or friends about the stalker. Ask them to watch for the person and tell the victim or the police if the stalker is seen.

Offer to go with the victim to and from school, work, and errands.

If you think the stalker is following you, don't drive to the victim's house. Drive to the nearest police station, fire station, bank, or hospital and get help.

If the victim must go to the police or appear in court, go with the victim. It will be easier if the victim knows she or he is not alone.

How Stalking Could Affect You

You may know the person who is stalking your friend or loved one. The stalker may try to convince you that the victim is going through a hard time or not being reasonable. Many people who become stalkers can present clever arguments. No matter what this person says, you must not accept any letters, gifts, or messages for the victim. Resist the temptation to feel sorry for this person. You cannot support both the victim and the stalker.

In Canada, charges of stalking can be brought at any time the victim has a "reasonable fear" for safety. This includes the victim's own safety and that of people the victim knows.

Sometimes friends and relatives of stalking victims may be in danger themselves. As you try to help this person remain safe, be aware of your own surroundings. If the stalker gets no response from the victim, harming the victim's loved ones may get a response. Also, you may be placed in a position of physically defending your friend. This is admirable, but you could put yourself in danger. Only get involved physically if it's an emergency and there is no time to call the police.

Get counseling help for yourself if you need it. You may be confused or frightened by what is happening to your friend or loved one. A counselor can help you sort out your feelings and decide how you can best help your friend.

Points to Consider

What do you think is the best way for a friend or relative to help a stalking victim? Explain.

How should a friend or loved one react if contacted by the stalker?

Should friends or relatives feel responsible to protect a stalking victim from violence? Explain.

Stalking laws and devices such as electronic monitoring help to protect victims of stalking.

Community members can help create better services for victims of domestic violence such as stalking.

Many organizations are helping to improve protection programs for stalking victims.

There are many Internet resources for law enforcement people, counselors, and victims of stalking.

Groups help to educate people in dealing with stalkers and their victims.

Chapter **6**

Protecting Victims of Stalking

Vince had dated Rochelle since ninth grade. He always

PAUL AND VINCE, AGE 19

thought they would get married. Then, Rochelle announced that she wouldn't see him anymore. Vince was torn apart. For weeks he tried to call her, but Rochelle wouldn't talk with him. His sadness turned to anger. He decided he wanted to get even.

Vince told his friend Paul about his anger. Paul worked to get Vince to forget about it. He said that lashing out against Rochelle would only make them both miserable. It wouldn't change anything. For weeks, Paul hung out with Vince. They ate out a lot.

When Vince wanted to talk about Rochelle, Paul always listened. In time, Vince began to date other girls. He realized that he and Rochelle were not meant to be together.

Improved Laws and Methods

Every American state has created laws that deal with stalkers. Canada has incorporated antistalking laws in its national criminal code. Police, judges, and attorneys can use these laws to protect stalking victims. Because the laws are new, it may be helpful for victims to get a copy of local statutes. In many cases, these laws may be obtained from victims' assistance agencies.

Many people sent to jail for stalking serve only a portion of their original sentence. This may happen because prisons have more inmates than they can handle. However, an electronic monitoring system now helps police track stalkers when they are released. The stalker wears a transmitter that tells a central monitoring center where the stalker is. The transmitter also can sense if the stalker tries to remove it. Another receiver in the victim's home provides a warning if the stalker is nearby.

"When I was stalked, I decided to take a self-defense class. It wasn't so much about being able to fight off an attacker. My class taught me a lot about becoming aware of my surroundings and avoiding confrontations."—Marnie, age 16

Helping All Victims of Stalking

It is likely that your community has many services for stalking victims. If not, you and your friends and family can help develop some. Schools, social service programs, churches, and hospitals are good sources of help. Find out what programs they offer for victims of stalking or domestic violence. With the help of these institutions, you may be able to organize presentations to help victims of stalking. Such presentations might include law enforcement people. Community members can attend these presentations and can ask questions and make comments about stalking.

Local women's groups and other service agencies may publish information in their newsletters about new approaches to helping victims. Local newspapers, television stations, and radio stations often print or air promotional articles as a public service.

Internet Resources

You can find information and resources about stalking on the Internet. For example, the Antistalking Web Site offers useful information on different types of stalkers. It describes how to remain safe from various types of violent behavior. It gives suggestions and referrals for agency help. You can learn about the latest studies on stalking as well as upcoming educational conferences and media reports. You can find this and other resources in the Useful Addresses and Internet Sites section on page 62.

National Efforts Against Stalking

One example of a service that helps victims is Project: Protect. This nonprofit women's group based in Chicago helps stalking and domestic violence victims. One of the greatest challenges facing this group is helping women in serious danger to relocate to other places. The project works to gain government help in creating new national programs for protection of stalking victims and their children.

Points to Consider

Why might a copy of local stalking statutes be helpful for a victim?

Do you think electronic monitoring of convicted stalkers keeps victims safe? Why or why not?

Do you think it's better to look for help from the Internet or from a live person? Why?

What other efforts do you think would help victims of stalking?

Glossary

abuse (uh-BYOOSS)—physical or emotional mistreatment

assault (uh-SAWLT)—a threat or an attempt to harm someone physically

criminal harassment (KRIM-uh-nuhl huh-RASS-muhnt)—a Canadian term for stalking

delusion (di-LOO-zhuhn)—a false belief

documentation (dok-yuh-muhn-TAY-shuhn)—a written record of something

domestic violence (duh-MESS-tik VYE-uh-luhnss)—violence that occurs at home or among family members

harassment (huh-RASS-muhnt)—the constant annoyance of someone

intermediary (in-tur-MEE-dee-er-ee)—someone who goes between two people with items or information

intimidation (in-tim-uh-DAY-shuhn)—an attempt to get someone to obey through threats or bullying

probation (proh-BAY-shuhn)—the time a convicted criminal spends out of jail under the close supervision of a court-appointed officer

psychopathic (sye-kuh-PATH-ik)—mentally ill; a person who is psychopathic is likely to become violent or dangerous.

restraining order (ri-STRAYN-ing OR-dur)—a legal order for one person to keep away from another

statute (STACH-oot)—a law

vandalism (VAN-duhl-izm)—needless destruction or damage to other people's property

vengeful (VENJ-fuhl)—having a desire to get even with a person believed to have caused harm

For More Information

Gedatus, Gus. *Date and Acquaintance Rape.* Mankato, MN: Capstone, 2000.

Havelin, Kate. *Sexual Harassment: "This Doesn't Feel Right!"* Mankato, MN: Capstone, 2000.

Nash, Carol R. *Sexual Harassment: What Teens Should Know.* Springfield, NJ: Enslow, 1996.

Rue, Nancy N. *Everything You Need to Know About Abusive Relationships.* New York: Rosen, 1998.

Useful Addresses and Internet Sites

Canadian Resource Center for Victims of
Crime
141 Catherine Street, Suite 100
Ottawa, ON K2P 1C3
CANADA

National Center for Victims of Crime
2111 Wilson Boulevard Northwest, Suite 300
Arlington, VA 22201
1-800-FYI-CALL (394-2225)
www.ncvc.org

Antistalking Web Site
www.antistalking.com
Resources for police, counselors, and teachers,
as well as victims of stalkers

Family Violence Prevention Fund
www.fvpf.org/index.html
Quizzes, information, and links to sites that
deal with domestic abuse, including stalking

World Wide Legal Information Association
www.wwlia.org/fun.htm
Canadian legal information for young people,
including definitions of law terms and links to
other sites

Youth Crime Watch of America
www.ycwa.org
Helps teens work to reduce crime at school and
in the community

Index

Index continued